Train To Red Cloud

A Small Boy's Journey

by

Barbara Heise Grooman

Writers Club Press

San Jose New York Lincoln Shanghai

Published by Writers Club Press, an imprint of iUniverse.com, Inc.

iUniverse.com, Inc.
620 North 48th Street
Suite 201
Lincoln NE 68504-3467
www.iuniverse.com

URL: http://www.writersclub.com

Dedicated to the memory of George Miller Wells
and his sisters
Sophie, Frieda and Florence Mueller

ACKNOWLEDGEMENTS

There are many without whose help this story could not have been written. My thanks to family members, some of whom hadn't seen or heard from me in years, who put up with my many questions, recounted tales they were told as children, rummaged in attics and scrapbooks looking for photographs and old documents.

Thanks also to Mr. Victor Remer, archivist at the Children's Aid Society who provided documentation of my uncle's trip to Nebraska; to Ann Siemer of Immanuel Lutheran Church, NYC, who located baptism certificates for Sophie and Frieda; Sister Francis Marie of Mount St. Francis, Peekskill, New York, who is still helping me search for Florence; and to Mary Ellen Johnson, Director of the Orphan Train Heritage Society of America, Inc. and her intern, Ashlee Thompson, without whose encouragement I would not have undertaken the task of publishing this book.

INTRODUCTION

When I began compiling information for a family tree I had no intention of writing a book, at least not one that would be released to the reading public. Who is going to buy or borrow a book that isn't filled with adventure, mystery or scandal? At best I hoped that some members of my family would be interested enough in their roots to at least skim the pages of anything I put together. So it was that I started my little project.

That was 20 years ago. What I had assumed would be an easy task turned into an all consuming passion. The mystery surrounding young Christian's separation from his family was one I was determined to solve. In gathering clues and following many false leads I discovered much about myself, particularly my stubbornness which obviously I inherited from my indomitable grandmother Sophie. As the pile of correspondence with orphanages, cemeteries and churches grew, so did my list of friends. I say this in all seriousness, for I consider my friends those patient church secretaries, orphanage archivists, cemetery superintendents and countless others who, while not always able to help me, offered words of encouragement and further clues.

While I never met Christian, now known to the world as George, I did correspond with him over a period of two years and was filled with love and admiration for him. The story of how I finally pieced together his life's story is the subject of yet another book meant either to encourage struggling amateur genealogists such as I, or to serve as a warning to those just beginning their search who expect overnight success. It is truly a "comedy of errors." Perseverance and a sense of humor are essential if you are to find your elusive ancestors.

One may ask if the results of my search were worth the effort. I emphatically reply "yes." This story of hope, determination, sadness, joy and fulfillment is one that any family can be proud to have in their album of treasured recollections. It serves as a reminder of just how good life really is and what one can make of it despite setbacks or detours.

It is with pride, not vanity, that I publish this story, in the hope that others will come to know and appreciate the likes of this man and his sisters. If you are as fortunate as I, you may have someone like my little Train Rider in your family. Perhaps reading this story will inspire you to share his or her story with the rest of the world.

CHAPTER 1

"Oma, Oma, guess what?"

Oma, comfortably stretched out on the chaise reading, peered over the top of her newspaper as her granddaughter, pony tail bouncing and feet barely touching the ground, came flying around the corner of the house. Before Oma knew what hit her, this bundle of energy called Caitlin threw herself onto her lap.

"You'll never guess in a million years. It's, like, unbelievable."

"If that's the case, you'd better tell me right now. A million years is a long time, especially if I'm not going to guess anyway. Let me set aside this paper that you've managed to crumple, you get more comfortable on my lap, and tell me all about it. Whatever it is."

Oma needed to regain some of her composure before hearing the big news of the day. You never knew what this imaginative child might come up with next, so it was best to be seated at attention, ready to be shocked, disapproving or genuinely pleased.

"Since you're sitting us today, you are the first in the family to hear the good news. This is the greatest thing that has ever happened to me. And it's just the beginning."

"Just the beginning of what? And please stop squirming."

"I got the part, I got the part." Unable to sit still any longer, Caitlin jumped to her feet and started singing "Tomorrow, Tomorrow."

Oma was slightly befuddled. "What part, and what are you doing tomorrow?"

"Oh, Oma. I told you I was trying out for the part of Annie in the school's winter musical production. I am Annie. The cast was announced today and I have the lead. Can I go in and call Mom and Dad at work to tell them?"

Permission granted, the excited 10 year-old ran into the house, leaving Oma to catch her breath and reflect upon Caitlin's good fortune. This little girl was a born actress and mimic who loved to put on shows for family, friends and anyone else who might buy a ticket to one of her performances. This chance to star in a real show was a dream come true. The silence was short lived as Caitlin's younger brother, Tyler, appeared in view.

"Hi, Oma. What's with Caitlin? She ran from the bus stop so fast nobody could keep up with her."

"Great news, Tyler. Caitlin is going to be the star of the school's winter production of the show Annie".

"So what's so great about that? And who's Annie?"

In as few words as possible, since Tyler didn't care for lengthy explanations of anything, Oma outlined the story of the little orphan girl who found herself a new rich Daddy and made life better for all the children in the orphanage.

"Caitlin an orphan? That's perfect. Serves her right."

Apparently Tyler had lost something in the telling of the story.

"What do you mean, serves her right?"

"Caitlin told me I was adopted, which means I was an orphan - one of those raggedy kids who beg in the streets. Now she can find out what it's like to be an orphan - sort of."

"Hey, Tyler. Caitlin was only kidding about your being adopted, you were never an orphan, and besides, all orphans aren't raggedy kids hanging out on the streets. Let's go inside for a snack and I'll tell you about an orphan in my life."

"You knew an orphan? Cool. Can I have ice cream and strawberries while you tell the story? I'm hungry."

Oma eased herself up from the lounge, put her hand on Tyler's shoulder and replied, "Sounds like a winner to me. Let's go."

CHAPTER 2

In the house Caitlin was just finishing up her conversations with her parents. Whether they had managed to make heads or tails of her rapid fire conversation was doubtful, but they had told her how happy they were for her and anxious to hear the whole story when they got home from work.

"So, Caitlin, I hear you're going to be an orphan," commented Tyler as he headed for the refrigerator and his after school snack.

"No, I'm not going to be an orphan; I'm going to act the part of an orphan. And I will be on a real stage and there'll be a huge audience and everybody will just love me."

"So what do you know about orphans? How does an orphan act?"

"Silly. Everybody knows that orphans are kids who don't have parents. Some of them live in dreadful orphanages or, even worse, just on the streets and sleep in alleys. They're dirty and poor and they beg for food. And what are you doing in the fridge?"

"I'm getting some ice cream and boy, are you wrong about orphans. Oma knows an orphan and she is going to tell me all about him. Or is your orphan a girl, Oma?"

Oma, who by now had settled herself at the kitchen table with a cool drink in preparation for the story telling session, smiled and replied,

"Actually there are four orphans in my life - three girls and a boy. Caitlin, if you can stop dancing around for a few

minutes, why don't you sit with us and listen. The story may give you some ideas on how to play the part of Annie."

Her curiosity aroused, Caitlin accepted the invitation. It couldn't hurt to listen and she might pick up some tips on being the perfect orphan Annie.

"The story begins on a cool, sunny day in September, 1902 in New York City as 12-year-old Sophie was making her way home from school. Most children are anxious to get home, have a little snack like you're having now, and go outside to play with friends. Right?"

The children nodded in agreement. Coming home in the afternoon was a lot better than heading out to school in the morning.

"Well, it wasn't like that for Sophie. She wasn't headed for the little apartment where her mother, sister Frieda, and little brother Christian would be waiting for her. That apartment had been empty for months. Instead she was headed for her aunt and uncle's place of business - a laundry and dry cleaning establishment. She wouldn't have a snack and most certainly wouldn't be allowed to go out to play. There was a lot of work to be done - sorting clothes, ironing, folding and even perhaps delivering clean laundry to customers. Her work there done, she would climb the stairs to the apartment over the store and help her aunt at supper time, do her homework and fall into bed, exhausted."

"Why did she go there? Why didn't she go to her mother?" asked both Tyler and Caitlin at the same moment.

"The children's mother had died earlier that year and their father couldn't care for them by himself. Sophie, the eldest, was strong and capable of helping but her young sister, Frieda had a problem with one of her legs and was in a great deal of pain so there wasn't much she could do around the house. The only boy in the family was 7 year-old Christian. There isn't much a boy that young can do to help out, and he certainly couldn't be left alone in a small apartment

in a busy city. It might have been easier if they were living in the country somewhere. Their father, whose name also was Christian, loved all his children, but he just didn't know how to manage without his wife whom he missed very much. And, he needed to find work. In his grief and desperation he had turned to his sister Anna for help. He asked her to care for his children for a few weeks while he left the city to find work. He had hopes of finding work and a home for his family in upper New York state."

"Oma, you forgot someone. You said there were three orphan girls. Who was the third?"

Tyler had been listening intently and realized almost immediately that the numbers weren't adding up. This young man didn't miss a trick.

"I didn't forget. It's just that the third girl, whose name was Florence, had hardly ever lived with the family. She was very frail and sickly from birth. No one really knows what the problem was, but as a tiny girl she was sent to a hospital to live. The children's mother, whose name was Theresa, was weak and in poor health, couldn't take care of a sick baby. Sophie, Frieda and Christian knew they had a little sister somewhere but they weren't sure where.

"Anna didn't really want to be responsible for these children but had agreed to keep them for a few weeks. If keeping them for this short time would assure that her brother and children would move away she decided it was worth the effort. The weeks turned into months and there was no word from brother Christian. Anna grew more angry and the children were frightened , but they kept hoping that their father would find a good job and come to take them away soon. In the meantime they did their best to please their aunt and uncle. They knew they were lucky to have a roof over their heads. There were many children in those days who weren't as lucky and they could be seen out on the streets, homeless and frightened. Yes, children, some orphans led lives like that, but not all of them.

"It was on this September day that Sophie's life fell apart. Frieda's leg was getting worse and she had a lot of trouble getting around. She wasn't even attending school with Sophie and she was of no use in the laundry. Any chore, no matter how small, was too difficult for her. Sophie hated leaving her home alone where the only attention she would get was comments about how useless she was. Both girls were more lonely than you can imagine. The one bright spot in their lives was Christian, their brother. As long as they stuck together, they knew that one day they would have a better, happier life. Their father would return, they would have their own little home with plenty of love to go around.

"When Sophie returned home from school this day neither her sister nor her brother were waiting for her in their living quarters. In a panic, Sophie ran downstairs.

'Tante Anna, Tante Anna, Frieda and Christian are not in our room. Where are they? What has happened?'

At this point Tyler interrupted. "What's Tante mean?"

Oma explained that Tante was the German name for Aunt, just as Oma is the name for Grandmother.

"I didn't know that. I thought your name was Oma."

"Actually my name is Barbara. See, you have learned something of a new language today."

"Sophie, get hold of yourself. A proper young lady doesn't run in here crying and carrying on. What will the customers think? Put on your apron and get in the back room. There's work to be done."

"Please, Tante Anna, you know where they are. Please tell me."

"They're gone and you are not to ask any more questions."

"But where and why", sobbed Sophie who was now very frightened.

"Why? You ask why? It's plain to see that I can't have a crippled girl and a boisterous boy around here. You're lucky you are old enough and strong enough to help me here, or you'd be gone too. I have my own family to care for, much less the children of my foolish brother. As long as you earn your keep you can stay here. Now that's the end of it. Get to work."

"With tears running down her cheeks, Sophie did as she was told. It wouldn't do to get her aunt any angrier with her. Perhaps if she worked hard and was obedient, the aunt would tell her more later.

"The days dragged into weeks and still no further information from her aunt. Every night Sophie, exhausted and lonely, fell into bed and cried herself to sleep only to dream about her sisters, brother and father. Always she was crying out to them but they never heard her. Where were they?

"Then, at the end of the second week of longing and pain, there was a moment of joy. Sophie came home from school to find that Frieda was there in the little room they had shared since their mother's death. She looked tired and pale and there were bandages on her leg, but she was there! A miracle. Sophie burst into tears of joy and relief. Frieda put out her arms and Sophie ran to her.

When the hugging, it felt so good to be hugged, and tears ended, Sophie had a hundred questions to ask. Of course the first question was, 'and where is our little brother? He came with you didn't he?' Frieda grew silent for a moment, took a deep breath and related the events of the past weeks. Some of the joy in the reunion disappeared as the story unfolded.

"On the fateful day, so etched in Sophie's memory, a Mrs. Witter who was a missionary from the Beekman Hill Church had come to talk with Tante Anna. Frieda had no idea what they talked about. All she knew was that when the conversation ended, her aunt and Mrs. Witter had come into her room and told her that she and her brother were going on a trip. The idea of a trip wasn't so bad. It would be pleasant to get away from the laundry. When Frieda asked if Sophie would be going too, her question was ignored. Apparently Aunt Anna had known about the trip before Mrs. Witter had appeared for the children's valises were already packed. In less time than it takes to tell, Frieda and Christian were taken away by the kindly missionary. While anxious about her sister, Frieda took comfort in the fact that at least her little brother was with her. She was sure that Sophie would join them.

"All Frieda remembered of the first place she and Christian visited was that it was big and very busy. There were pleasant men and women talking to groups of children. These children were all shapes and sizes. Some looked frightened, some were crying, some looked relieved and almost happy, and, of course, there were those who were loud and acting very important. Frieda and Christian weren't frightened, but very puzzled. They were seated on a bench outside a group of offices and told to wait - they would be called in to talk to someone about their trip. Frieda was called in first, leaving Christian there in the hallway. That was the last Frieda was to see of him

"After being ushered into a room where a gentle, soft-spoken lady was waiting for her, things happened very quickly. Frieda was having such difficulty walking, it became quite apparent she wasn't up to a trip anywhere but to a hospital! Frieda was admitted to the Hospital for Crippled Children. She was examined by doctors who told her that she would have surgery that would take away the pain but that she would always walk with a limp. It was a good thing these doctors saw her when they did. If they hadn't, she might have lost that leg. What worried Frieda was, that though she would be better, she was very much alone. She had no idea where Christian was going on his trip, and Sophie didn't know where she was. What would become of her after the operation?

"To Frieda's joy and amazement, as she was recovering from the operation and worrying about her future, her father appeared on the scene. The good news was that he had come to sign papers to get her released, but the bad news was that she would have to live with Tante Anna again. Her father still did not have a real home for her.

"After hearing this story, Sophie hugged Frieda even tighter and whispered, 'Sister Frieda, we are together again and that is good. And as soon as we can, we will find our little brother and sister and be a family again. Let's make a pact right now. We will not give up until we find them.'

Oma stretched and looked at her watch. "Good grief, look at the time. Your parents will be here any minute. Time for me to pack up and head home to my children, (these children being Oma's three somewhat spoiled cats who ruled supreme in her little apartment).

"First, Oma," pleaded Caitlin who was looking a little teary eyed, "tell us what happens. Do the sisters get the family back together? How does it turn out?"

Before Oma could reply, Tyler commented, "well, it's a pretty good story. How do you make all that stuff up?"

Oma's response to them was, "No time to finish the story now. And, Tyler, you're forgetting what I told you earlier. This is a true story."

"If it's really true, it's cool. But how do you know it's true?"

With a wistful sigh, Oma replied, "Because brave young Sophie was my *Oma. It was she who first told me the story. And I hear your dad's car in the driveway so I must be off. Give me a hug. I'll see you again soon and I'll tell you the rest of the story."*

CHAPTER 3

The raspy sound of Oma's door buzzer startled the cats who ran in three directions in something of a panic.

Oma grinned and commented as she headed for the door. "It's O.K., kids. It's just Tyler and Caitlin. They're going to visit with us for an hour or so while their Mom and Dad run some errands. It will be fun having some company this rainy, dreary day."

When Oma opened the door she was surprised to see her oldest granddaughter, Jennifer, also.

"Jenn, this is a pleasant surprise. I thought you'd be hanging out at your house or visiting one of your friends."

"Well, Mom and Dad said they were going to take the kids out to eat after they pick them up here, so I decided I'd come along, too. You know me, I like eating out. And besides, I wanted to see your new cat. And I can always use your computer while you're telling stories to the kids."

It must be noted here that, although only a few years older than her siblings, she considered them "kids" and, of course, she was too grownup for story telling sessions. Knowing this, Oma was flattered. It wasn't often that this young lady was willing to hang out with her. The above mentioned kids had already entered the apartment and were tracking down the cats. They laughed at Wally perched atop the refrigerator, imperiously surveying his domain, peeked in the closet where Boo was hiding and offered her words of encouragement, and then scooped up little Moochie who hadn't run very far and loved being stroked.

The greetings over there followed the ritual of pouring drinks and putting out a tray of chips and other assorted goodies. The younger children then announced they were ready to hear the rest of the story, although Tyler reminded Oma he was still not convinced this was a true story.

"Where did we leave off?" asked Oma as she settled herself in her rocking chair.

"I know, I know!" announced Caitlin. "Sophie and Frieda, those are strange names, have made an oath to find their brother and sister."

"Yeah," chimed in Tyler. "But we don't know what happened to Christian after he got separated from his sister, whatever her name was."

He's interested, thought Oma, but he doesn't want to appear too interested. She also noted that Jenn had not left for the computer room. Though not sitting in the story circle, she was still in the room, crooning to Moochie, but obviously listening.

"O.K., gang, let's go back to New York City in the year 1902, where young Christian was left sitting in a waiting room at the Children's Aid Society.

"Christian was frightened but trying hard not to show it. He was used to a lot of attention and he had never been left alone like this. His Mama, when she was alive, always wanted him near her. He was her only son and she was so proud of him. She was too ill and frail to take him out to play or to do many things for him, but his sisters had always stepped in to amuse him and play with him. Papa, too, had always been proud of him and enjoyed showing him off to his friends and family. But after Mama died, something seemed to have died within Papa also. He wasn't around much anymore and Christian had grown more dependent upon his sisters. And now he was alone. Sophie didn't even know that he had left the house, and Frieda had disappeared behind a closed door down the hall. He felt like crying, but knew that 7 year-old boys did not cry. He must be brave. Frieda would come back, or, better yet, his Papa would come to get him, saying this had been a big mistake. He did not like this trip that Tante Anna had planned for him.

'Hey, kid, what's your name?'

"Christian looked up into the face of a grinning, freckle faced boy who must have been about 12 years old."

'Christian George Mueller,' he replied.

'What kind of a name is that? My name's Joey, and I'm an orphan, just like you.'

'I'm not an orphan. I have a papa and three sisters. And I am Christian in honor of my father, and George in honor of one of my grandfathers.'

"Christian did not want to be called an orphan. He had a family, he had a house to live in, he wasn't dirty and ragged. He didn't know what this place was, but he knew he did not belong there.

'Shucks, kid, don't get huffy. Maybe you have a papa, but I guess he don't want you. Else you wouldn't be here. Me, I'm happy to be here. Gonna get on one of those trains and go West. No more of this beggin' and bein' chased by policemen. Soon as I get me a family out there I'll go out on my own and see Indians, maybe join the army or somethin'. Lot better than this dirty city.'

"Christian didn't want to appear ignorant, but what was this boy talking about? Trains, the West, and Indians? He didn't want to see the West, he wanted his sisters and his papa. He liked New York. He knew nothing else.

'I think there has been a mistake. What is this place and what do you mean about going West?'

"Flattered at having someone look to him for answers, Joey took on a somewhat fatherly expression and sat down beside bewildered Christian.

'Chris, can I call you Chris? This here is the Children's Aid Society. Some guy named Charlie Brace got this idea that us poor kids in the city, with no families to look after us, would have a good chance of a better life out West. So he got this group together and started sending trainloads of kids West to find new homes and families. Guess it has worked out pretty good, been doing it for more than 50 years now.'

"Somewhat puzzled, Christian asked, 'Who brought you here?'

'Nobody brought me. I don't have anybody that cares enough to bring me. I just decided that I'm sick of living in the streets and being hungry most of the time, so I came here by myself. I figger they'll be glad to have me out West. I'm strong, can work and I don't look too bad. Somebody will want me, and even if it don't work out, at least I'll be out of this place.'

"Before Christian could ask any more questions of this source of knowledge, he heard his name being called. He looked up to see a gentleman with a sheaf of papers in his hand standing outside the door closest to his bench. 'Christian Miller, please come here.'

"Christian jumped up and said, 'I'm here, Sir, but my name is pronounced Mewler and I write it Miiler.'

"The gentleman looked a bit puzzled at first and then looked at his papers again. 'Ah, I see, it is a good German name. In German it is Muller with a funny mark over the u, called an umlaut. It does sort of look like Miiler. Here in New York we don't use that funny umlaut so we could spell it Mueller, but it is easier to just call you Miller. Come in, young man. I want to talk to you.'

"As Christian rose from his seat, Joey grinned and said, 'Good luck, Chris, whatever your last name is. Maybe I'll see you out West.'

"Christian followed the man whom, for want of a better name, we will call Mr. Smith, into a small office furnished with two chairs and a large desk covered with papers and more papers. It looked as though Mr. Smith had had a very busy day.

'Welcome to Children's Aid Society, Christian. We are happy to have you here and even happier that we are going to be able to help you. You are going to go on a long trip, see new places, and find a family.'

'But, Mr. Smith, I don't want to go on a trip to see new places. I don't need to find a family. I have a papa and three sisters . I don't need another family.' "Christian was trying hard not to cry.

'Well, Chris, it says here,' and Mr. Smith pointed to one of the many papers on his desk, 'it says here that your mother has died, your father has fallen on hard times, and your aunt just can't take care of you properly. You need a new mama and papa who can care for you and who will love you.'

"Chris felt his throat tighten. Oh, how he wanted to cry. Maybe he had lost his mama, but his papa loved him, he knew he did. And he had sisters who loved him. Why must he go West? No words came out, there was nothing he could say to this man.

"Mr. Smith continued, 'You are going to have a chance for a wonderful new life. You're going to live where there is good, clean, fresh air, and kind people. It will be a new life for you. And a good one. Now, here's the plan. You will spend the night here where you will have a good supper and a comfortable bed. To-morrow you will go to a farm and school we have over on Staten Island and spend a couple of weeks learning about life in the country. Then you will board a big train and take a great trip. At the end of the line will be a new home and new parents for you. Trust me, Chris, this is going to be good.'

"Chris pondered this briefly and decided it didn't sound too bad as long as sister Frieda would go with him. He then had the courage to ask, 'Frieda is going with me. Right? She is just in the other room talking to someone. The two of us will have a new family. Right?'

"Startled, Mr. Smith thumbed through the papers on his desk and then replied, 'Well, Chris, we've found that your sister has a medical problem. Right now she is not well enough to make the trip. She is going to a hospital to make things better.'

'So, can I wait until she is better and then the two of us can go together?'

'Chris, I can make no promises. I do know that we will do everything to find you a home and bring your sister back to good health. Now, I am going to call someone to take you to supper and find you a bed for the night. Sleep well, and try not to worry.'

"There was nothing else for this little boy to say. He trusted Mr. Smith, but he wasn't at all sure of what the future held for him. Tired and hungry, he gratefully followed Mr. Smith out of the office. Perhaps after dinner and a good night's sleep things would look brighter. He had to put this day out of his mind and think about tomorrow. Tomorrow had to be better."

At this point, Caitlin jumped up. "That's where the song, Tomorrow, *came from!"*

"Caitlin," commented Jenn from her seat in the corner, "don't be silly. In real life orphans didn't go around singing about tomorrow. Get real."

Tyler chimed in, "Yeah, Caitlin, get real."

Caitlin looked a little deflated so Oma tried to reassure her. "I'll bet that when Caitlin sings this song now she'll have a better understanding of an orphan's hopes and will do a great job of singing it."

Conversation was interrupted by the old cuckoo clock announcing the hour. It was time for the children to get ready to leave. As they hugged and said their good-byes, Oma said, "Enjoy your dinner and have a good night's sleep."

"Just like Christian." Tyler commented.

"Not just like Christian," said Jenn very wisely. "We know where we are going to be tomorrow." And with that, the children ran out the door to greet their parents.

CHAPTER 4

All too quickly the summer passed. The children were back in school and busy. Jennifer, now a high school freshman, was excited about the swim team , homecoming and driver's ed. Tyler was back in baseball, sometime playing first base and sometime, joy of joys, catching. Caitlin had started re-hearsing for Annie. *In other words, life was hectic on the home front. Family gatherings had become less frequent and for the time being at least, the story of Christian was on hold.*

It wasn't until a glorious Indian Summer October evening that the whole family managed to gather for a birthday cook-out held in honor of Oma's birthday. Following the feast of ribs and all the good fixings that go with them, the grownups were enjoying a few moments of relative quiet while the chil-dren were out walking the dog. They had been promised more cake and the continuation of the story of young Christian upon their return.

"What's this story you've been telling the kids?" asked Tim. "Whatever it is, I'm surprised that they're all so inter-ested in it."

"It's the true story of my great-uncle George's life. Each of the kids has a special reason for being so interested. Tyler is quite taken by this tale of an orphan boy. Caitlin is think-ing in terms of portraying an orphan on stage. And I think Jenn sees herself in the role of the eldest child, responsible for the 'kids'."

Tim, like his son Tyler, seemed a little skeptical, but his wife Karen, who loved a good story and had a keen sense of history, appeared genuinely interested.

"Where and how did you get all the facts to come up with this story?"

"Well, Karen, you know what a compulsive amateur genealogist I am. Once I heard what little was known of uncle George, I became determined to find out the whole story. It has taken me 20 years to piece it together. I've tracked down birth certificates, death certificates, and newspaper articles. I've been in touch with the Children's Aid Society and the Orphan Train Heritage Society. I've been in contact with archivists and church secretaries who, remarkably, took an interest in the story as it developed and became allies in my search. It's a remarkable story and I feel compelled to share it."

"Do you mean there was really an aunt who would treat her nieces and nephews that way? Sounds like a fairy tale to me," commented Tim.

"All the characters are real. Of course I can't know for sure what motivated Aunt Anna to treat the children that way. There's no one left to tell her side of the story, but I do know that thousands of children like Christian, for whatever reasons, were either totally abandoned or placed in orphanages during that time in history. For some of them there were happy endings, for others there was just more unhappiness and loneliness."

"So, how did things turn out for your uncle?"

Oma smiled and replied, "For the 'rest of the story', just sit where you are and listen. I hear the kids coming. It's time for the next chapter. Why don't you build us a little campfire and join the story circle?"

More curious than he cared to admit, Tim agreed to get a fire going while the kids brought out the marshmallows and gathered twigs to toast them on. It was a perfect evening for a crackling fire and a good story. Oma looked lovingly upon her little family and thought to herself, "Uncle George, how you would have loved an evening like this."

CHAPTER 5

As they sat carefully tending the marshmallows, Tyler asked, "Oma, can you finish the story about your Orphan Train Rider tonight? I've kind of been thinking about Christian and want to know now just what happened."

"I've been thinking about him, too," chimed in Caitlin. "And since I've been Annie I also think about his sisters. Tell us some more."

"Actually, I'd like to hear more about him, too," commented Jennifer. "That's because I have to write a paper about welfare and stuff like that, and some of this history would be helpful."

Oma suspected that Jenn didn't want to appear too interested in story time and that conducting research offered the proper excuse for sitting at Oma's knee with the "kids".

"Following a night of dreams about his family, Christian was wakened quite early by the sounds of voices and much activity as his roommates dressed and washed up for breakfast. His dormitory type bedroom had seemed crowded but when he followed the group to the dining room he was amazed. So many tables, so many children, so much confusion. Where had they all come from and why was he here? When would Papa come to rescue him? After they had finished a hearty breakfast, one of the adults who seemed to be in charge of the activities stood up to make an announcement.

'Children, I know some of you may be a little confused and are wondering what is going to happen next. I'm here to tell you that life is going to be very good for you. You are going to leave this crowded, dirty city and go to homes out in the country where there are people waiting for children like you to become part of their families. You older children will be taught trades and learn to make your own way. Younger children will have the chance for schooling, and most importantly, have new parents to look out for you. You won't be lonely or afraid anymore.'

"Christian wasn't sure he understood all that this man was saying, and he wasn't really interested. He liked the city, he had a family, and he knew he wouldn't be going anywhere on any old train, but being a polite little boy, he didn't speak out. He was sure this man meant well and he didn't want to upset him.

"After listening to this little speech, Christian was taken with a group of children to the Society's summer place, Bath Beach on Long Island Sound. At one time this had been an exclusive summer place for some New Yorkers. Now one of the buildings, close to the famous Coney Island, had become a part of the Society where children were looked after and screened before their trip West. For some children this place, away from the noise and smells of the city, must have seemed like heaven. To Christian it was just a lonely time away from his family. He stayed there two weeks and then was taken to a place called Kensico Farm Training School, a small farm where children could learn something about life in the country. There were gardens and livestock to care for. Even a seven year-old could learn something of what life in the real country would be like, if he was looking forward to life in the country that is. Christian definitely was not looking forward to it.

"Shy and frightened, though he didn't admit it, Christian kept pretty much to himself, but he did finally form a friendship with a boy about his age, named Willie. Neither of them joined groups of other children at play time but sat on the sidelines just watching the activities. As they overcame their natural shyness they talked with one another about their lives and the mistake that had been made in sending them to this place. They were sure they would be returned to their families and would continue to see one another right here in New York city.

"And then, a few weeks later, their hopes were dashed when it was announced they would be leaving the next morning on a train headed west. No parents had come to claim them and take them home. They really had been abandoned. They were being sent away from all they knew and loved. They were to be Orphan Train Riders. Right then and there they made a pact.

'No matter where we go, we will stick together. If someone wants one of us, they have to take both of us. We are like brothers.'

"At the station the next day there was a lot of hoopla as the children boarded the train. There were photographers shooting pictures of the group, some of the children were cheering and waving, obviously excited at the prospect of a new life. Others, like Christian and Willie, were fighting back tears as they stood there in their Sunday best having their pictures taken. For some of the children there were family members who had come to wish them well on their journey. Some of them were crying at the thought of the separation, others were apparently happy, whether it was relief at getting rid of a child or a genuine belief that the child would have a better life, we do not know. Willie and Christian had no one there. They were very much alone except for one another. It seemed that no one cared for or about them. Would someone out there in the West really welcome or want them?"

Oma paused in her story. "It's getting late. I guess we'd better stop here."

In one voice the "kids" and Jenn cried, "No, Oma. Keep going. We can't stop here. There's no school tomorrow. We can stay up late. Please, please."

Not wanting to get caught in the middle of a discussion about bedtime or chores, Oma glanced at her son and daughter-in-law, who nodded their approval of continuing the tale.

"O.K. Here's the deal. You all take your showers and get ready for bed. We'll finish the story inside over a second piece of birthday cake. It's getting a mite chilly out here."

As one, the children raced upstairs to ready themselves. Oma tried not to look smug as she thought to herself, "They're hooked. They really want to know about their great-great uncle." She rose from her chair, stretched and thought ahead to the next installment. She also noted that the parents of these eager children were sticking around, too. "If just one of this group cherishes this story as I do, it will continue to be told through future generations. That is as it should be."

CHAPTER 6

*In what seemed like no time at all, the children reappeared
with scrubbed and shining faces, second helpings of birthday
cake on their plates, and the announcement that they were
ready for the rest of the story. Oma settled back in her easy
chair and continued.*

"When the picture taking and good-byes were done, the children were helped aboard the train. There were other passengers
also boarding, but one car seemed to be just for the children. It
seemed to Christian that there were about 50 or 60 of them, enough
to fill up that car. They were boys and girls of all ages, toddlers to
teen-agers , with most of them being older than Christian and
Willie. They stuck together like glue and managed to get seated
together where they just sat back and watched all the activity.
They tried to make themselves as inconspicuous as possible. They
weren't old enough to join in the older kids' games and joking,
and not young enough to be tended by the older girls and the
escort from the Children's Aid Society. At home Christian had
been the baby - suddenly he was a little man but not feeling like it
on the inside.

"The train chugged out of the station and soon they were in
the Pennsylvania countryside. Christian had never been in the country except for his days at the training school. For awhile at least,
he gazed at the passing scenery with a sense of wonder, forgetting
the pain that had been with him for so many weeks. They passed
cornfields and orchards, observed horses working in the fields,
saw mounds of pumpkins waiting to be carved into jack-o-lan-

terns or turned into pies. It was a whole new world. Even the sound of the wheels speeding along on the track was soothing. 'Clickety-clack, clickety-clack, Christian Mueller, you're on the right track.'

"As the day wore on, Christian, like all young boys, grew weary of staring out the window and listening to the sound of the wheels. Hour after hour the children had to remain in their seats, their only exercise being the walk to the tiny toilet at the end of the car. They weren't treated badly - they were just so confined! The hours dragged on, and Christian heard someone say they were in Ohio. The train made some stops to let other passengers off but no orphans got off. On and on they went.

"Supper was served in their seats - sandwiches, milk and fresh fruit. Then it was time to go to sleep- in their seats. Christian slept fitfully and dreamed of his sisters and parents. And the train continued on and on through the night.

"Morning came early, the scenery was less interesting, and the song of the wheels on the tracks had become, "clickety-clack, clickety-clack, Christian Mueller, there's no going back.' Some of the other children said they were in the state of Indiana now, more than half way to some place called St. Louis, Missouri. He wondered if that was far west enough and if he would be getting off this train. He'd had enough of this traveling!

"They did reach St. Louis at the end of the second day, but that was not their destination. They had traveled 1005 miles but the end was not yet in sight. It was the end of the line for the Pennsylvania Railroad System. Here in St. Louis the Burlington Route would take over. As Christian ate his supper sandwich and prepared for another uncomfortable night in his seat, he was not aware of uncoupling cars or changing engines. He really wasn't interested in much of anything, but, he said to himself as he curled up to try to get some sleep, 'I would really like a bed.'

"There was excitement in the car the next morning. In about another 500 miles when the train stopped some of the children would be getting off the train. The first stop for this group of Orphan Train Riders was a place called Red Cloud, Nebraska. "That's a funny name ," commented Christian to Willie. 'I think it has something to do with an Indian,' replied Willie. That sent Christian's mind reeling. Would there be Indians at the train station?

"As the day wore on there was an undercurrent of excitement and fear throughout the car. Who would be getting off at Red Cloud? Who would be chosen? What were the people of Red Cloud like? Christian's stomach was tied up in a knot but he made himself eat his supper, another sandwich. He didn't want to seem ungrateful.

"Suddenly the train came to a screeching halt. Why? There was no train depot in sight. This couldn't be Red Cloud. The children were buzzing and growing anxious when they heard the announcement. There had been a derailment up ahead. They would be spending another night on the train as they waited for the track to be cleared. Their announced arrival would be a day late.

"Sleep did not come easily to any of the children that night. What would this delay do to their chances in Red Cloud? Who would be waiting for them? Would they have to go on ahead to another town? 'Clickety-clack, clickety-clack, there's no going back.' Even the older, braver teens were growing fearful.

"Needless to say, the train finally pulled in to Red Cloud, but they were a day late, and it was the wee hours of the morning. The children waited impatiently on board for their escorts to the center of town. A wagon finally arrived and only as many children that fit in that one wagon were taken to town. Luckily, Christian and Willie were among the chosen group. Hopefully, they would not have to spend another night on the train.

"The children were taken to a church in the center of town, just south of the court house, and ushered to a big platform where they were all lined up for prospective parents to look them over. Now, since the train had been delayed, there weren't as many people there as had been expected. Some people had driven many miles in their wagons and buggies the day before and just couldn't make the ride again.

"Christian and Willie sat up there on that platform side by side and reminded one another of their vow. They would go as one, no matter what. It so happened they were sitting in the front row of children, and sitting in the front row of prospective parents was a man by the name of Rees Thompson.

"Now this Mr. Thompson was there on a double mission. He was from the town of Cowles where he ran what they called a sand pit in addition to a small farm that provided food for him and his wife. The evening before the train's arrival he had run into his friend, Mr. Wells.

'I'm going to town tomorrow to fetch me a boy. Are you coming?'

"Mr. Wells replied, 'Well, I can't go back down. I drove my team down there today to be there, and they didn't come in. I can't drive them down again.'

"At that time he lived in the Eckley Community, about 15 miles from Red Cloud and so he just couldn't turn his team around and go back again.

'Do you want me to find you a boy?'

"And so, as a favor to Mr. Wells, Mr. Thompson was in Red Cloud looking for two boys. When the children were ushered in, he took one look at Christian and , thinking of his promise to his friend, said, 'I want that boy. He looks just like Doc Wells.' (Mr. Wells was known to friends and neighbors as "Doc".)

"When a gentleman came to take Christian from his seat, Christian took a deep breath and said, 'No, I won't go.'

"Mr. Thompson wasn't about to argue so he said, pointing to Willie, 'All right, I'll take him.'

'No,' said Willie rather defiantly.

"Somewhat amazed, Mr. Thompson and the representative from the Children's Aid Society had a brief discussion. It became clear to them that the boys were determined to stay together. Thus Mr. Thompson left the little church with Christian and Willie in tow. They looked at one another and grinned. They weren't in New York, but they were together and they would always be together. And when they went back to New York they would go together."

Oma paused, yawned and said, "Well, children, we've gotten Christian to Nebraska. Now I think it's time for you to go to bed."

"No, we have to find out what happens next. Did the boys stay together? What about Mr. Wells? You can't stop now."

"Tell you what," replied Oma. "If I can spend the night here, first thing in the morning we can finish the story."

And so Oma got to spend the night with her children - a welcome guest with a story to tell. Who could ask for anything more?

CHAPTER 7

Bright and early the next morning the children appeared at the breakfast table, ready for the next chapter in the life of Christian. Oma, armed with a steaming cup of coffee, gathered her wits about her and picked up where she had left off the night before.

"Christian and Willie tried not to appear impatient as they waited for Mr. Thompson to sign some papers and talk with the representative from the Society. While they had hoped against hope that they would never leave their families in New York, at least they had each other. Mr. Thompson seemed like a nice enough man and they were off that train! Things were looking up.

"Before heading for Mr. Thompson's place he announced they had to first stop at the general store to buy some supplies for his wife. This store was nothing like the stores they were accustomed to back in New York. When they had gone shopping back there they never visited just one store. They had gone to the bakery for bread, the butcher shop for meat, the poultry store for chicken and eggs, the delicatessen for sauerkraut and pickles. There had been candy stores which they visited on rare occasions, toy stores which they never got to visit but whose wondrous wares they viewed from the street with their noses pressed against the storefront window. From peddlers' wagons on the street they purchased vegetables, pots and pans and even clothing. In this store in this place so far from home, there was everything imaginable under one roof! And Mr. Thompson seemed determined to buy a little bit of everything from every corner. When he and the boys departed the premises their arms were loaded with packages and they were all beaming. Not only were there supplies for Mrs. Thompson, there were overalls, shirts and shoes for the boys.

'Can't have you youngsters lookin' like city folks' had been Mr. Thompson's comment as he had selected clothing appropriate for young farm boys. Though Willie and Christian were wearing their best clothes in order to make a good impression as they met prospective parents, having slept in them for three nights, they were wrinkled and dirty as well as out of place in this small country town. The new clothes looked strange to them, but they looked forward to being dressed in anything that would be clean and more comfortable.

'While we're at it, guess we'd better pick out a toy or two so you can entertain yourselves some of the time. Doc Wells and me aren't used to having youngsters around the place and we can't be amusing you all the time. We've got work to do.'

"Thanks to Mr. Thompson's generosity Christian became the proud owner of a set of toy soldiers and a spinning top. Willie chose a yo -yo and a bag of marbles. This was as good as Christmas and birthday rolled into one. What a day this was. Perhaps those people at the Society had been right. Life was good out West.

"As the clerk was tallying up and wrapping their purchases, Mr. Thompson couldn't help but notice how Willie and Christian were eyeing the candy jars on the counter.

'Looks like these boys each has a sweet tooth that needs nourishing. Better throw in a couple of licorice sticks and some jelly beans, Pete.'

"The clerk grinned as he filled two candy bags. Handing them to the boys he said, 'Here's your candy from my friend Mr. Thompson and a little extra from me. Welcome to Red Cloud, young fellas.'

"The boys were speechless but the look they gave one another clearly said, 'What a great day this is turning out to be.'

"On the drive to the Thompson farm they were all silent. Mr. Thompson was wondering what his wife's reaction would be when he pulled up with not one but two orphans. The boys were thinking of their benefactor's kindness and wondering what they would find on the farm. Would it be like the training place back in New York? And what would Mrs. Thompson think of them? What if she didn't approve of her husband's choices? And of course they were thinking of those they had left behind. Would they ever see them again?

"When Mrs. Thompson heard the wagon approaching she ran out to the porch to greet her husband and new son. But what was this? Two orphans? What had her husband up and done without consulting her?

"Mr. Thompson turned to the boys as the wagon came to a halt in front of the house. 'You just sit here for a minute while I talk to the Missus. I have to explain to her about having two fine young men with me instead of the one I promised.'

"So saying, Mr. Thompson jumped from the wagon and joined his wife on the porch. The boys held their breaths as they watched the grown-ups talking. Somehow they knew their fate now rested in the hands of this kind man. Could he convince his wife two sons were better than one?

"Apparently Mr. Thompson was as persuasive as kind. After just a short conversation, he and his wife came to the wagon, reached out their hands and said as one, 'Jump down out of there and come on inside.'

"While Mrs. Thompson had never been blessed with children of her own, she instinctively knew that here were two tired, dirty, bewildered and hungry children so she set about resolving all these problems as quickly as possible. Being a firm believer that cleanliness was next to Godliness she first saw to it that Mr. Thompson got out the tin bath tub, set it in the kitchen and filled it with the hot water heating on the back of the stove. The boys weren't at all sure how they felt about having a stranger bathe them, but the water did feel good and she was very businesslike as she set about scrubbing off the grime and soot. They were feeling relaxed and remembering mothers back in the city who had so often bathed and tended them. They had grown up a lot in just these few weeks, but it felt good to be babied once again.

'Tired as you must be, you're going to bed as soon as you have a good supper, so just slip into these nightshirts I found in your little valises. Just this one time you get to eat in your sleepwear. Most times there are still some chores to be done after supper, but tonight is special.'

"So saying, she left their nightshirts where they could reach them and left them to dry themselves off as she turned her attention to the large pot of soup also simmering on the big wood stove.

"The boys felt a little silly saying grace and eating supper while dressed for bed, but they had to admit to themselves that it all felt rather good. It was a good supper, their stomachs were full and they were safe.

"True to her word, Mrs. Thompson heard their bedtime prayers and tucked them into bed right after supper. She hugged them, kissed them each on the forehead and said, 'Sleep well, little ones.'

"Alone for the first time in many hours, the boys sat upright as soon as this good-hearted woman left the room. Tired as they were, they had to compare notes.

'Chris, what do you think? Aren't we the lucky ones? We're together. These people are kind. This is the most comfortable bed I've slept in ever so long. How about you? You and I will be best friends for life, won't we?'

"Christian didn't answer right away. Yes, he was relieved that the trip was over and that he had met such kind people. But he had not set aside the belief that one day he would be reunited with his sisters and father. Maybe Willie didn't have a family that would stand by him the way Christian's remaining family would. Maybe Willie didn't miss his old life. Willie had never really told him just how he had become an orphan or what his old life had been like. Christian suspected that Willie's life had been harder than his. He knew that he and Willie would be friends for life, but would they always be together?

'Yes, Willie, we are very lucky, and we will be friends for life,' was his response to his friend.

"To himself he thought as he snuggled under the covers ready for sleep, 'Friends for life. And when my family comes for me they will take you with me.'

CHAPTER 8

"It was barely daylight when Christian woke from the best sleep he'd had in weeks. He sat up, rubbed his eyes, and called out, 'Sophie, is it time to get up?'

"There was no response. As Christian opened his eyes he called out again, 'Sophie, is it time to get up?' Still no response.

"Christian looked about him and for a moment was confused. This was not his bed, this was not the room he shared with his sisters. Where was he and who was this strange boy in bed with him?

"Then it all came rushing back. He was in Nebraska. He had a temporary new home and this was Willie next to him. He heard Mrs. Thompson calling to them.

'Come on, you sleepy heads. The rooster's crowing, time to get up. Put on your clothes and get yourselves down here for breakfast. We have a busy day ahead of us.'

"There was no need for Christian to rouse Willie. Mrs. Thompson's call to arms had done that for him. The boys jumped out of bed, hastily donned the new clothes that had been laid out for them the night before, and rushed to the kitchen.

'Good morning, boys. Why, you're looking much better than you did yesterday evening. No more dark shadows under your eyes and you don't look so forlorn. A few days of good country cooking and there'll be more flesh on your bones. Yes, I can see that life here is going to agree with you. Now, let's eat.'

"And eat they did- steaming bowls of oatmeal, eggs, sausage, biscuits, applesauce, and plenty of cold, fresh milk. When Chris-

tian politely thanked his hostess for preparing such a grand breakfast for them on an ordinary weekday, she laughingly replied,
'Honey, this is the way we eat every morning. Here in the country
a man needs a good start before he tackles a day's work.'

"Mr. Thompson finished his meal before the others and
commented as he left the table, 'While you boys finish up I'll
go load the wagon. We're going to deliver some stuff to my
friend, Doc Wells.'

"Had Christian been paying strict attention he would have
noted that Mr. Thompson was loading , not only supplies for the
Well's farm, but also his little valise and packages from the general store. But since he hadn't been watching, he had no idea
what lay in store for him that day.

"It was a brisk autumn day, a good day for a ride. Mr. Thompson didn't seem to be in a hurry and let the horse amble on at
a leisurely pace. Unlike yesterday's ride spent in silence and wondering, today's ride was one of conversation and laughter. Mr.
Thompson asked about life in the city. He had never been more
than 20 miles from his farm so stories about trains and tall buildings and wonders such as the Brooklyn Bridge filled him with
amazement. He in turn told the boys tales of farming, harsh prairie
winters , and neighboring Indian tribes. All too soon they completed the three mile trip to the farm of Doc Wells.

"As they headed up the drive to the large farmhouse they
spotted a gentleman standing on the porch and waving. Doc Wells
must have been more anxious to see them than they to see him.

'Here we are, Doc. I've brought you the boy like I promised.'

"Willie and Christian were stunned. What was he saying? They
were delivering supplies, not a boy! Willie, ever the optimist, chose
to believe that Mr. Thompson meant he had brought two boys for
a visit. Christian, more of a realist, felt his heart sink. Mr. Thompson had lied. He didn't want two boys. He was going to give
away, or worse yet, sell one of them! He wanted to jump from the
wagon and run as fast as he could. There was no one he could
trust. He had to leave this place and find his way back to his

sisters and family. But he knew this was impossible, at least for now. He tried not to look frightened. He would not let anyone know what was going on in his mind.

"Once again the boys were left in the wagon as Mr. Thompson stepped down to have a conversation that would affect their lives forever. The two men talked briefly and then came to the side of the wagon. Both were smiling but looked a bit uneasy.

"Mr. Wells said, 'Boys, you may not know it, but I went to Red Cloud the other day to find me a son, but the train didn't make it to town that day and I had to come back home. Mr. Thompson here was able to go yesterday and promised me he'd find me a son. I've known him a long time and I trust him, so I knew I could count on him for this very important decision. When he saw you two he was impressed. He could see that you are as close as brothers and want to be together. He figured that if he told you right away that you wouldn't be living in the same house you'd refuse to go with him. So he played it smart and took both of you. Now, neither one of us can keep two boys, but we sure each want to have a son. We only live three miles apart so you could see one another every day or two. That's about as close as you could get, and we'd be mighty happy too. What do you say?'

"The boys listened and then asked permission to talk together about it alone. The adults agreed and walked away from the wagon, leaving the boys to come to a decision. Willie was the first to speak.

'Chris, I know this isn't turning out just like we thought it would, but it doesn't seem so bad. We won't be in the same house but we'll be closer than if we were still living in New York and didn't even know one another. These seem like good people. I want to stay. And something else, Chris, I haven't told you. I don't feel so good. I don't think I could stand getting back on that train again to look for another family. Some days my head hurts real bad and I get real scared. I'm so tired. But I'll do anything you say.'

"Christian wasn't sure he liked what he was hearing. His best, and perhaps only, friend was asking him to make a choice for him. Only 7 years old , he was now a decision maker. It wasn't fair. What were his options? He could lie to Willie, agree to stay and then run away at the first opportunity. What would that do to Willie? Remembering how he felt when his Papa left him behind, for whatever reason, he knew he could not do that to Willie. If he insisted that Willie return to the train with him he knew that it would be hard on his friend. Willie did look kind of weak and tired. How long could he last traveling from town to town in that train without becoming really sick? A little boy facing a big decision.

'You're right, Willie. This is the place to stay. Let's tell Mr. Thompson and Mr. Wells'

"That decision assured two little boys from New York new homes in Red Cloud, Nebraska. Since Mr. Thompson had noted immediately when he saw Christian that he bore a striking resemblance to his friend, Doc, it was understood that this was the boy who would stay at the Wells farm. Willie would remain as a member of the Thompson family.

"Life looked good, at least on the surface. The boys were with nice folks in comfortable homes, had plenty to eat and they were off that awful train. Willie was extremely happy. Christian was still a little dubious.

"It was just one week later that Christian's new life took an unexpected turn. He thought nothing of it when a horse and buggy carrying some neighbors whom he had not yet met turned into their driveway. He paid little attention as the man and woman were greeted by Mr. and Mrs. Wells and ushered into the house. He did notice that they seemed rather forlorn looking, but lots of grown-ups looked that way. He turned his attention back to his game of chasing the chickens around the coop. If he had known what the discussion in the house was about, he would have been a very worried and unhappy boy.

"These neighbors had come with a very sad story and request. It seems they had had a son, just about Christian's age, who had died just two weeks before Christian had come to live with Mr. and Mrs. Wells. They were lonely and distraught. They had decided they should have another boy and they had heard about Christian's arrival. They wanted to take him home to be the son they had lost. Now Mrs. Wells was known to be a very kind hearted woman. As she listened to their story she was deeply touched and decided it was only right that they should have this boy. It would be easier to give up Christian after only a week than it had been for this couple to lose a son they had loved and cherished for seven years.

"Once again, without understanding why, Christian was given up by someone who had cared for him, and turned over to strangers. He didn't argue or disagree as he was placed in the carriage with this couple and sent off to another new home. He was too tired to argue, and he knew it wouldn't do any good. He just hoped they didn't live too far away from Willie and the Thompsons.

"The remainder of the day became a blur in his memory. The people were kind, they gave him a good supper and he had a comfortable bed to sleep in. Perhaps that was all he had the right to expect in this life. He fell asleep and dreamed of the 'clickety-clack' of the train. He was no longer a passenger on an orphan train, but he was still on a journey that led he knew not where.

CHAPTER 9

"The sun had barely risen and Christian was still half asleep when he heard the clattering of a horse's hooves in the driveway. He groggily stumbled to the window and saw a white horse drawing a buggy come into the yard. It was Mr. and Mr. Wells! They had come to claim Christian. They could not let him go. In the week they had known him they had come to love him as much as any parents could love a child. It was the love, not the length of time that mattered. Christian ran down the stairs to greet them, tears of joy running down his cheeks. They wanted him, they loved him, they had come to take him home. He wasn't an orphan anymore.

"Some days later as Mr. Wells and Christian were in the chicken coop gathering eggs from some rather feisty hens, Doc said to the boy, 'I've been thinking a lot about you and your name. You have a fine name, Christian George Mueller, and I don't want to take anything away from you, but I have an idea. George is a common name in my family and my wife's name, before she married me, was Alpha Miller. Now it seems to me that a good proper name for you would be George Miller Wells. That way you still have your grandfather George's name, not to mention my name, and Mueller out here would be pronounced Miller, so Miller would be your father's name as well as the name of my wife's parents. What do you think?'

"Christian didn't have to think very long. George and Alpha Miller Wells were kind and loving parents and he would be proud to have their name. He would never forget his natural parents, but he had a new life now so his name should be new also. From that day on he was known to his family and the community as George Miller Wells. It wasn't until he turned 21 that the courts would acknowledge an official adoption, but that didn't matter. What mattered was the love he felt for his new parents and the love they felt for him.

"True to their word, George and Rees saw to it that young George and Willie got to see one another two or three times a week. Willie was happy in the Thompson home and even happier to be so close to his best friend. Life was good. Or was it? Christian, now George, spent enough time with his friend to know that all was not well. Willie admitted to him, and only to him, that the headaches had not gone away but had actually become worse. The pain became so severe and his head felt so heavy that he began having trouble holding it up. He never complained to his new parents but it finally became evident to all around him that something was wrong. He was taken to the local doctor who was baffled by these symptoms. The Thompsons contacted the Society hoping that perhaps they knew something of Willie's medical history that would provide an answer to what was wrong. The Society could offer no clue so they sent out an agent to visit Willie and offer advice as to what might be done. One look at Willie and it was apparent that Willie needed medical attention that could not be provided in the small town of Red Cloud. Arrangements were made to take him back to New York for examination and treatment. George heard the man say that as soon as Willie was well, he would come back to the Thompsons.

"Alpha and George took young George to the train station to say goodbye to his friend and to wish him well. George couldn't keep back the tears as he hugged Willie.

'Don't cry, Chris. Oh, I forgot, your name is George now. Don't cry. Those doctors in New York will fix me up and I'll be back sooner than you think. And here, while I'm gone I want you to take care of these for me. Remember when we went shopping with Mr. Thompson and he let us buy some toys? Well, I want you to hold on to my yo-yo and marbles for me while I'm gone. I can't play with them in the hospital so you might as well play with them while I'm gone. I'll be back to get them soon.'

"George never saw Willie again. He never understood the whole story but what he heard was that even as they traveled to New York Willie became totally blind. No one in Red Cloud ever knew what the diagnosis was, but they did learn that young Willie died shortly after being admitted to the hospital. Alpha and George broke the news to George as gently as they could. He seemed to take the news very bravely, but for many a night he cried himself to sleep thinking of his friend who planned one day to return to New York. He had returned and he had died. He thought of his father who had simply disappeared in New York, and of his sisters still in New York who had apparently forgotten him. It was then that he put aside any ideas of returning to the city of his birth. There was nothing there for him. He was George Miller Wells of Nebraska. Christian George Mueller of New York City no longer existed.

"Well, children. It's time for me to pack up and get back to my place. Heaven only knows what my kids have been up to since I stayed away so long."

"Oma, that can't be the end of the story! What about the sisters in New York? Did they really forget their brother? What became of little George's natural father? There must be more!"

"Of course there's more", replied Oma. "I just wasn't sure how much more you wanted to hear. I can tell you about George's baseball career, his music, his inventions and the reunion."

"Did you say baseball career?' piped up Tyler, the Little Leaguer. "What position did he play?"

"He was a well known center fielder and substitute catcher."

"Music? Was he an entertainer like me?' asked Caitlin.

"I think his musical career was limited to family gatherings."

"Inventions? He must have been a good student," commented Jennifer, the studious granddaughter.

"His inventions didn't make him famous, but they made life on the farm much easier."

"Reunion?" Sentimental, teary-eyed Karen looked wistful and hopeful. "Do you mean was reunited with his sisters?"

"Surprising, but true."

"Well," commented Tim the doubting one, "seems to me there has to be another installment. When will you finish the story, Mom?"

Oma smiled and replied, "We'll be together for Thanksgiving. I'll finish the story and even bring photos and letters to prove that this has all been fact, not fiction. Now, I must be off."

As she drove back to her home Oma smiled to herself. Yes, she would tell them the "rest of the story", a story of hope, determination and love.

CHAPTER 10

"That turkey sure smells good and I'm starved. I don't know how much longer I can wait to eat," commented Tyler as he entered the kitchen where his mother and Oma were putting the finishing touches on what promised to be a splendid Thanksgiving feast.

"Judging from the looks of that bird, I estimate his time of arrival at the table to be in about 30 minutes", said Oma laughingly. "I think you can hang on that long. Why don't we all go into the living room in front of that nice fire and finish the story of our Orphan Train Rider while we wait."

"Good idea. I'll get Jenn and Caitlin."

"While you're rounding them up I'll get us some punch and a little something to munch on to ease those hunger pangs."

Within a few minutes they were all seated in front of the fireplace and ready for the final chapter of this story that had been so long in the telling.

"George missed his friend Willie terribly and would never forget him, but as the weeks passed so did the aching in his heart. Time does heal our pain.

"George attended the little school there in the Eckley community, helped his new parents with chores around the farm and found that he really liked life in the country. In fact, he found it much more to his liking than life in the noise and bustle of the city.

"It came as something of a surprise when Doc announced in the autumn of the following year that he was selling the farm and buying the hardware store in Cowles, a nearby town. And so it was that Doc Wells the farmer became Doc Wells, businessman.

This move shaped the rest of young George's life, for it was here in Cowles, helping Doc in the family business , that it was discovered that though George didn't care much for formal schooling, he did have a knack for things mechanical. He loved being in the store and eagerly watched Doc at work repairing tools and implements. One day George would not only repair things but would also invent things. He was only in his late teens when he invented a hay "self stacker" and an automatic washing machine. Around town he came to be known as a mechanical genius.

"Life wasn't all work. George enjoyed playing ball with his friends and also learned to play the trombone. On one visit to the Wells family, Miss Bogardus of the Children's Aid Society, reported that she had enjoyed an evening of listening to George play his trombone while his father played the coronet and his mother the piano. It was a happy family and Doc and Mrs. Wells firmly believed there was no better boy in Nebraska than their son George.

"As the years passed, George's memory of his three sisters dimmed. In fact, he couldn't picture their faces anymore. He had resigned himself to the fact that he would never see them again when, as he approached his teen-age years, he received the biggest surprise of his life - a letter from Sophie, delivered by Miss Bogardus! "

"I knew it, I just knew it!" shrieked Caitlin with joy. "I knew she'd find him. How did she do it, Oma?"

"Sorry, kids", announced Tim before Oma could answer. "It's time to eat. Oma will have to finish the story later."

It was Caitlin who offered to ask the blessing at the dinner table. She concluded her words of thanks for all the good things the family had shared with "And thank you for looking out for our Great-Great Uncle George and his family. Amen."

Portrait of Sophie

Portrait of Frieda

CHAPTER 11

It was now early evening. Following a meal that every-one declared was the best they had ever eaten, they had set to work cleaning up the kitchen and then taken a brisk walk around the block. Now they were gathered again in the living room waiting for the conclusion of the story.

"This is it, Oma. We're not going to let you stop for any-thing. You have to finish the story tonight," ordered Caitlin as she curled up in her father's lap.

Oma nodded and continued the tale.

"Things had not been easy for Sophie and Frieda after George's disappearance. Aunt Anna was less than pleased that Frieda had returned. She had really wanted that 'cripple' out of her life but she doubted that she could find a way of doing it. Her brother Christian had been distraught when he had signed the papers releasing the children to the Children's Aid Society. He had come to his senses in time to get Frieda out of the hospital but there had been nothing he could do about his young son who by then was on his way West. He made Anna promise not to send his daughters away. He in turn promised to come for them just as soon as he found a good job.

"Where Christian went looking for work is unknown, but Anna took it upon herself to tell the girls that he had gone far north to Maine. No one knew if that was the truth or not. Anna would say nothing more on the subject of Christian's whereabouts.

"The one good thing that had come of Frieda's being sent away was the surgery. As the doctor had promised, the pain was gone and she could get around again. True, one leg was shorter than the other and she had to wear a special shoe, but she could get around. Despite any problems in life she might have to face, she seemed blessed with an inner goodness and joy, always looking for the best in everything. If things didn't go well one day she wouldn't brood about it. She looked ahead to the next day which was bound to be better."

"Like Annie," commented the little actress.

"Sophie on the other hand seemed to take life more seriously. She had been deeply hurt and could not set the pain aside. As the oldest child she also felt it her responsibility to hold the family together. For the time being she would have to tolerate life with Aunt Anna, but as soon as she was old enough to take care of herself she would set about making things right again.

"As the girls grew older and completed as much schooling as they were to receive, they were of more use to Anna in the family business. Frieda became especially good at sewing which finally led to her finding a position in a private home as a domestic. Eventually her skill as a seamstress led her to a position in the home of a very wealthy family outside the city. Her quality of life was improving.

"Sophie continued working for her aunt until she finally learned where her sister Florence was living. No one to this day is quite sure where the institution was located, but Sophie always referred to it as 'St. Joseph's.' Eager to be near her little sister, Sophie went to work there as a maid. She had a roof over her head, could visit her sister every day, was treated kindly by the nuns, and no longer had to put up with her unloving relatives. All that remained for her to do was find her father and brother.

"Her sister had been found in an orphanage. Perhaps young Christian was somewhere here in the city as well. In what free time Sophie had, she made the rounds of New York city's many orphanages with no luck. She had just about come to the end of her list of places to visit when she finally came up with a clue. A kindly clerk at the New York Foundling Home asked if Sophie had contacted the Children's Aid Society. This had not been on the list of her places to visit, but she would follow any lead. She didn't realize at that moment that she had found the place where Christian's long journey had started.

"It wasn't customary for the Society to give out much information concerning the children they had placed, but she was persistent. She learned that George was in Red Cloud and the promise was made that Miss Bogardus would take a letter to him when she made her next trip West. It might take awhile before they would see each other, but at least they could communicate through letters."

CHAPTER 12

"Back in Cowles, George didn't know what to think as he read his sister's letter. He was mighty happy to hear from her but he wasn't sure just how to reply. He used to dream about being reunited with his family, but his family was here now, and even if he wanted to leave them there was no way he could. Train fare was expensive and he had no money that was his own, at least not right now. A reunion would have to wait.

"George replied as best he could, and thus began a correspondence that would continue for many years. Through these letters he learned that his sister Sophie's life had taken a turn for the better and she was a happy young woman, happier than she could ever remember being. For starters, she had met a wonderful young man by the name of Wilhelm Schirmer. Sophie told George that he was the kindest, tallest and handsomest man she had ever laid eyes on. It had been love at first sight and within just a few months they were making plans to marry. And there was more good news. She had heard from their father who was now living in Putnam County in New York state where he was working in, of all places, a dry cleaning establishment. Sophie made her father promise that after she and Wilhelm were married he would come and live with them. All was right with the world.

"Then, just as suddenly as they had started, the letters stopped. It was months before George heard from his sister again. This time much of the news was sad. Sister Florence had died in April and had been buried alongside her mother. Spring turned into a hot and miserable summer, one of the hottest on record in that part of the country. Sophie had been saddened by the death of her sister but had come to accept it for she had always suspected that this frail child would not grow to womanhood. Then came another crushing blow. While everyone was striving to escape the terrible heat, Christian continued to labor in the dry cleaning establishment. It was too much for him to bear. He became just one of the many who died in the heat that summer. And so it was that Sophie laid this troubled man to rest with his wife and youngest daughter.

"Had it not been for the love of Wilhelm, Sophie would have completely fallen apart. She had failed to bring her family together, but she and Wilhelm would have children and give to them all the love that had been denied Sophie as a child. They were married in November, 1911 and settled into a little apartment in New Jersey, across the river from the city where Sophie had known so much unhappiness. She would not look back. With Wilhelm at her side she would only look to tomorrow.

"A year after her marriage Sophie wrote George to tell him that she and Wilhelm were the proud parents of a darling little girl, named Frieda in honor of their sister. He, who was once an orphan, was now an uncle.

"George reported that things were going well for him and he was being trained to take over his father's hardware and repair business. In preparation for his responsibilities he spent the winter of 1913 working in a large machine shop in Kansas. It was in that same winter that Sophie gave birth to another daughter, Elizabeth. In their letters to one another they continued to talk of a reunion. They didn't know when, but they knew it would happen.

"The following year brought the beginning of what was to become World War I and life became somewhat uncertain. People wondered if the United States would become involved in the war. Sophie and Wilhelm moved back to the city where Wilhelm began working in a government job at the docks.

"Despite the threat of war, things were going well for George. He reported that in April, 1916, just before he turned 21, he was legally adopted by George and Alpha Wells. They had always considered him their son but had never formalized the adoption. He was now officially George Miller Wells. His joy at the adoption was quickly overshadowed by the death of his mother a few months later. While she wasn't his natural mother, he had known and loved her for 14 years, twice as long as he had known Theresa Mueller. He was still working with his father when he met, courted and married the lovely Helen McTaggart. After their marriage George decided they should strike out on their own. He bought property in Wilsonville and took up farming again.

"This is about the time he became quite serious about baseball. He had fallen in love with the game from the first time he was big enough to pick up a bat and the highlight of his career came when he played on the Cowles team with Charles 'Dazzy' Vance. George usually played center field but often was called upon to be substitute catcher for Cowles. Dazzy was a well known pitcher, noted for his unannounced fast balls. George took great pride in the fact that he was catcher for Dazzy in the last game he pitched before he went to play for the Brooklyn Dodgers. On that day the Cowles team beat Red Cloud 3-2. Dazzy went on to the Baseball Hall of Fame. George was left with crooked fingers that he was sure were caused by Dazzy's fast balls.

"Sophie's letters continued to bring both good and bad news. She and Wilhelm were thrilled when they had their third child, Wilhelm Jr., an heir to carry on the Schirmer name. But once again tragedy struck. In February, 1919, within one week of one another, Wilhelm and Wilhelm Jr. died. The cause of death of the father was pneumonia and heart failure. The official cause of death of little Wilhelm was acute gastroenteritis and dehydration. Sophie was convinced her little son died of a broken heart, grieving for his father. Sophie was devastated. Her grief was such that she could scarcely get out of bed. Thankfully, her sister Frieda stepped in, caring for Sophie and her daughters and encouraging Sophie to pull herself together and carry on. She must not give in to the grief and risk losing her daughters as her father had. Desperately in need of work to support herself and her daughters, Sophie returned to Aunt Anna's dry cleaning establishment. It might not have been the best place to work, but she could bring the girls with her and keep an eye on them as she labored. Life was playing cruel tricks on her.

"The years flew by and still there was no reunion. Frieda married, was blessed with three children, and then was widowed. Sophie remarried and she, her new husband John and her girls, moved to a small farm in Connecticut in search of a more peaceful existence. It was here that their daughters Helen and Martha were born.

"Meanwhile back in Nebraska, at the request of his father, George had returned to Cowles to help run the family hardware business. Doc assured his son that upon his death the business would be his and signed a paper stating this. With George back on the scene Doc decided now was the time to go on a visit to the mountains with his new wife. While on a trip to the mountains he had longed all his life to see, Doc Wells died. To further complicate things at this very same time, George came down with typhoid fever and was bedridden for weeks. These were dark days. He had scarcely recovered when there came a dispute with his step-mother about the family business and, rather than become involved in a quarrel, he left the business to his step-mother and bought another farm on the outskirts of town. He and Helen were content there but longed to have a child so in 1927 they adopted a baby boy whom they named Dean. He was to be their only child, and they adored him. They might not be prosperous business people in town, but they were a happy family.

"Finally in the early 1940's Sophie and Frieda decided the time was right for a reunion with their brother. It had been 40 years since the three had last been together. Their children were grown, life had become a little easier. It was now or never!"

CHAPTER 13

Oma's audience had appeared dumbfounded as the story unfolded. When they heard the word "reunion" they just about exploded. The story was going to have a happy ending.

"How did it go? Did they recognize one another?"

"I know for a fact they were reunited. I can't begin to tell you how it went or what they did. So I have with me Uncle George's own words, taken down in an interview when he was a very old man. He became very well known in Red Cloud after his return there in 1936 when he gave up the farm. He worked as a town employee for many years and then, when most men retire, he started an equipment repair business. Everybody in town knew George Wells and when he turned 85 he was interviewed by some newspaper reporters. Now remember as I read this to you that these are the recollections of an old man and some of it may seem a bit odd, but it is the way he remembered it. He doesn't say much about his sisters' visits to Red Cloud, but he certainly had a lot to say about his trip to New York."

"He went back to New York?"

"Yes, one trip, and quite a trip it was. Now here are his words"

Oma picked up a sheaf of papers and began to read:

"They came back and forth and visited me for, oh three or four times…then in 1948 I decided to go, I was going on back there. So Helen and I went back to New York, and to see them and then we went around to the cemetery where my mother was buried….One of my sisters lived at Pleasantville, New York. She had made arrangements and bought transportation from a railway company so we could get up in the morning, go down to the depot and get on a train anytime we wanted to. Every fifteen minutes a train went through so we could get out pretty near any time we wanted to and we could go wherever we wanted to go. We covered all over New York. Every day we went someplace and spent the whole day. All the carfare and everything. We didn't have to worry about anything like that. So we spent all the time we was there traveling back and forth in New York. So we went to see some of my aunts and cousins that was there. Some of my aunts was there, but this one aunt, I don't think we got to see her. She didn't show up…"

Oma set aside the papers and gazed fondly at her audience. For the moment at least they all seemed speechless.

"There's just one last thing I'd like to read to you. These words were written by a very kind gentleman, Victor Remer, who works for the Children's Aid Society now and was a great help as I researched the story of Uncle George. Without ever knowing George, he was able to say, 'It is a remarkable story of a fine young man who overcame the formidable obstacles of surrender by his father, separation from his sisters, removal to strange new surroundings and new foster parents. He must have been a scared and angry child—yet he grew to be a fine, responsible, productive and loving adult and parent. It is a mark of his character and we understand why you are all so proud of him. He was lucky, too, in having been placed with Mr. and Mrs. Wells, who loved and nurtured him.'

"I'm only sorry that I didn't complete the story before Uncle George's death. I think he would have been pleased to know about you, and perhaps he would have found comfort in the fact that I finally located the institution where his sister Florence spent her years before her death. I just re-

cently learned that she spent those years at St. Joseph's Hospital for Consumptives. So now we know she died of tuberculosis as her mother had. Frieda died in 1968, and Sophie died in 1975. His dear wife, Helen, became frail and had to be placed in a nursing home where he visited her regularly, even though she had lost all memory of him. I suspect she may have suffered from Alzheimer's Disease. Uncle George died in September 1984, and, very sadly, his son died just 11 days later. Aunt Helen lived on for 4 more years without understanding that her husband and son had passed on before her. All of the brave heroes of this story are gone now, but what a story they have left behind. A story that can make us proud."

As they listened they all nodded in agreement. Then Jenn spoke up.

"I'm proud of great-great uncle George, but I'm just as proud of great-great aunt Frieda and great-grandmother Sophie. I've learned enough in school about women's rights and roles in society to realize that they were very brave in times that weren't easy for women. Coming from a family like that, it's no wonder you're so feisty, Oma."

Not to be outdone, Tyler had something to say as well.

"When you first started this story I thought you were making something up. I guess you've proven that it's for real. It kind of makes me proud to know about such a neat guy. Do you think I'm such a good ball player because of him?"

"And I'll be the best Annie ever," chimed in Caitlin, at which everyone laughed. Leave it to Caitlin to get in the last word.

The Reunion, August, 1942

Dean, Helen, Sophie and George

The George Wells Family

Helen and George were proud of Dean who served his country during the Korean War

EPILOGUE

It is December and the grand production of Annie has drawn to a close. It is time for curtain calls. When the young star of the show is handed a bouquet of roses amid much applause she raises her hand for silence. With poise and grace beyond her years she speaks.

"Thank you all very much. This is a very proud moment for me. If I did a good job in this role it's because I didn't just rehearse and learn lines. I learned about real orphans in my very own family. And so I would like to say thank you especially to great-great Tante Frieda, great-great Oma Sophie and great-great uncle George who taught me what "tomorrow" is all about."

Not everyone in the audience quite understands what this little speech is all about but Oma sits back in her seat, tears streaming down her cheeks.

"George, Sophie, Frieda and little Florence, this one's for you."